PUMPKIN CARVING STENCILS

30 HALLOWEEN PATTERNS FOR PAINTING AND PUMKIN CRAFTS

Pumpkin Carving Stencils
© Hello Halloween Press
First Edition, November 2019

Published by:
Hello Halloween Press

HOW TO USE:

STEP 1:
Cut or tear out your chosen design.

STEP 2:
Tape paper design onto your pumpkin where you would like it to appear.

Tip: Choose the flattest surface of your pumpkin for your design.

STEP 3:
Trace your design onto your pumpkin by going over the stencil lines with a pin tool (nail, pen tip, needle, etc.), poking holes about 1/8" apart. You can connect the holes with a marker or pen to make the design more visible for carving.

STEP 4.
Refer to the pattern to locate areas requiring carving; use a skinny, serrated crafts knife to slice along the nail holes outlining these areas. The black area of each design is the area that should be cut out. Be careful not to cut the reverse!

STEP 5:
Insert a candle into your pumpkin and watch your design come to life!

SOLID BLACK AREA = CUT OUT AREA

SOLID BLACK AREA = CUT OUT AREA

SOLID BLACK AREA = CUT OUT AREA

SOLID BLACK AREA = CUT OUT AREA

SOLID BLACK AREA = CUT OUT AREA

SOLID BLACK AREA = CUT OUT AREA

SOLID BLACK AREA = CUT OUT AREA

SOLID BLACK AREA = CUT OUT AREA

SOLID BLACK AREA = CUT OUT AREA

SOLID BLACK AREA = CUT OUT AREA

SOLID BLACK AREA = CUT OUT AREA

SOLID BLACK AREA = CUT OUT AREA

SOLID BLACK AREA = CUT OUT AREA

SOLID BLACK AREA = CUT OUT AREA

1 2 3
4 5

SOLID BLACK AREA = CUT OUT AREA

67890

SOLID BLACK AREA = CUT OUT AREA

SOLID BLACK AREA = CUT OUT AREA

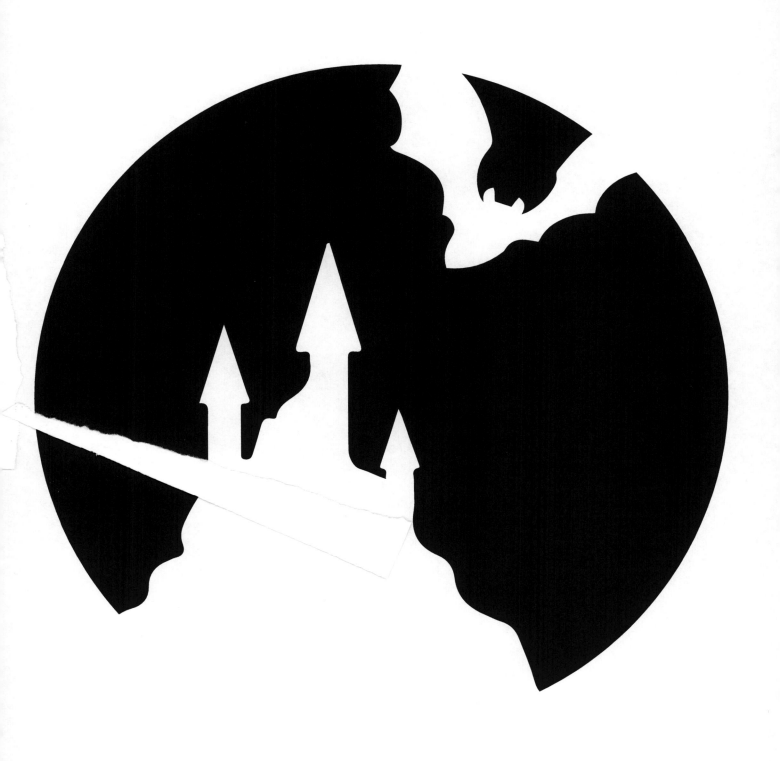

SOLID BLACK AREA = CUT OUT AREA

SOLID BLACK AREA = CUT OUT AREA

SOLID BLACK AREA = CUT OUT AREA

SOLID BLACK AREA = CUT OUT AREA

SOLID BLACK AREA = CUT OUT AREA

SOLID BLACK AREA = CUT OUT AREA

SOLID BLACK AREA = CUT OUT AREA

SOLID BLACK AREA = CUT OUT AREA

SOLID BLACK AREA = CUT OUT AREA

Made in the USA
Middletown, DE
19 October 2020